One Two One

Thanks to
Richard Barham, Joan & Gene Barnard, Robin Cannon,
Iain Dale, Kim Dewdney, John Gammons, Genesis Laboratory,
Mark George, Helen Hirons, Nick Carew Hunt, Rupert Otten,
Sally & Liam Lawrence-Smith, Alan Samson, John Simmons,
Sheila Smith, Antony Tiernan, Hanneke van der Werf, Julia Wigg,
and all Members of Parliament who generously gave time and
encouragement to One Two One.

First published in Great Britain
in 1998 by: Politico's Publishing
                                     8 Artillery Row, Westminster, London, SW1P 1RZ

Designed & produced by: System Colour Ltd.
                                     9 Heathmans Road, Fulham, London, SW6 4TF

Printed by: G & B Printers.
                                     Gomer Place, Teddington, Middlesex, TW11 9AR

ISBN: 1902301013

One Two One

Women In Parliament

Photographs

Victoria Carew Hunt

breakthrough
breast cancer

Message from Breakthrough

Breakthrough Breast Cancer is a charity committed to funding research to discover what causes breast cancer, how it can be prevented, and to develop new treatments so that ultimately the disease can be eradicated.

Breakthrough is also establishing the first centre in the UK wholly dedicated to breast cancer research, in partnership with the Institute of Cancer Research. When this new centre -The Breakthrough Toby Robins Breast Cancer Research Centre at the Institute of Cancer Research - opens for business in summer 1998, it will bring together leading scientists to focus on the disease.

Breakthrough Breast Cancer
Summer 1998

For information about the different ways of donating to Breakthrough Breast Cancer or enquiries about the charity please telephone (0171) 405 5111

To make a donation cheques should be made payable to 'Breakthrough Breast Cancer' and sent to Breakthrough Breast Cancer, PO Box 7012, London E1 8AZ

Kodak Limited are a major supplier of X-ray film for mammography,
supplying hospitals and breast screening units throughout the UK.
Our thanks go to Kodak Health Imaging for their support with this project.

The Speaker

FOREWORD

This is the 25th anniversary of my election to Westminster. The election of May 1997, in bringing more women than ever before to the House of Commons, is one of the highlights and most rewarding moments of these years.

It is most fitting that Breakthrough Breast Cancer has been involved in the publication of these photographs. I applaud this and the great work that the charity is doing in the fight against breast cancer.

My fellow Members of Parliament from all the parties should be congratulated for contributing their time and well-considered words of wisdom to this cause. They have achieved a great deal. This is their book.

Betty Boothroyd

Speaker

Betty Boothroyd, Member of Parliament, West Bromwich West

"If at first you don't succeed
Try, try, try again"
Irene Adams, Member of Parliament, Paisley North

"All women become like their mothers. That is their tragedy. No man does. That is his"
A Woman Of No Importance, Oscar Wilde
Janet Anderson, Member of Parliament, Rossendale & Darwen

"Progress is not about being progressive, but actually moving forward"
Bertolt Brecht
Hilary Armstrong, Member of Parliament, North West Durham

"Don't let others limit you any more than you limit yourself"
Candy Atherton, Member of Parliament, Falmouth & Camborne

"The language of priorities is the religion of socialism"
Aneurin Bevan

Charlotte Atkins
Member of Parliament
Staffordshire Moorlands

" 'That none shall be enslaved by poverty, ignorance or conformity' part of the preamble to my party's constitution. I don't believe anyone can fulfil their potential unless they have a good start in the early years and good quality education
The happiest people I meet in my constituency tend to be the children at school, nursery or play-group
Sometimes I envy their innocence and joy"
Jackie Ballard
Member of Parliament
Taunton

"Not shouting about our successes doesn't mean we aren't achieving them"
The Rt Hon Margaret Beckett, Member of Parliament, Derby South

"God grant me the serenity to accept the things I cannot change, courage to change the things I can and the wisdom always to tell the difference"
Slaughterhouse Five, Kurt Vonnegut
Anne Begg, Member of Parliament, Aberdeen South

"The one important thing I have learned over the years is the difference
between taking one's work seriously and taking one's self seriously
The first is imperative and the second is disastrous"
Margot Fonteyn
Elizabeth Blackman, Member of Parliament, Erewash

*"Our lives shall not be
sweated from birth until life closes.
Hearts starve as well as bodies.
Give us bread, but give us roses"*
Bread and Roses, James Oppenheim
Hazel Blears
Member of Parliament
Salford

"Growing numbers of women suffer from breast cancer; it is the disease of our generation.
We must ensure all patients receive the best possible treatment"
The Rt Hon Virginia Bottomley, Member of Parliament, South West Surrey

"Life's…a tale
Told by an idiot, full of sound and fury,
Signifying nothing"
Macbeth, William Shakespeare
Helen Brinton, Member of Parliament, Peterborough

"Smile at us, pay us, pass us; but do not quite forget. For we are the people of England, that have never spoken yet"
The Secret People, G K Chesterton
Angela Browning, Member of Parliament, Tiverton and Honiton

"One should try everything once except incest and folk dancing"
W.C. Fields
Karen Buck, Member of Parliament, Regents Park & Kensington North

"What we have to learn to do, we learn by doing"
Aristotle
Christine Butler, Member of Parliament, Castle Point

"All of us, all human beings have the same set of DNA <u>addresses</u>, but not necessarily the same <u>contents</u> of these addresses. That is the main reason why we are all different from each other"
The Blind Watchmaker
Richard Dawkins
"Dawkins' welcome reminder is reinforced by constituency visits to the wide diversity of people who live and work in Cambridge. From people with learning disabilities to a hi-tech product launch, my bicycle as well as the DNA provides the connection"

Anne Campbell
Member of Parliament
Cambridge

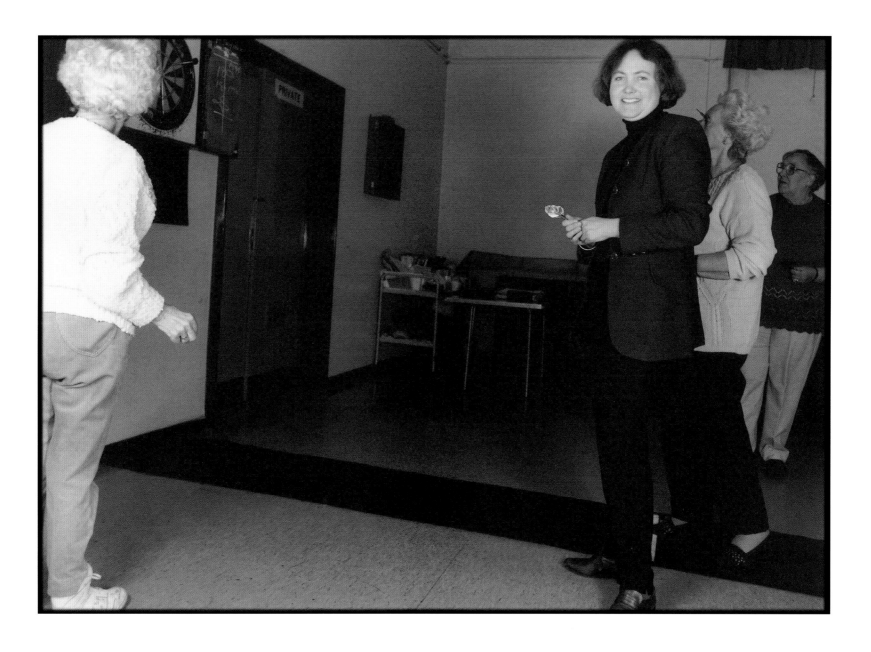

"Community centres in Dagenham are a hub of activity with short-mat bowls, line dancing, snooker and other games. Today it's Ladies' Darts and it's a great way to meet constituents informally"
Judith Church, Member of Parliament, Dagenham

"Counting the numbers of elected women should not become a substitute for analysing where the power lies in our society and insisting on democratic accountability"
Linda Clark, Member of Parliament, Edinburgh Pentlands

"All my reporting life, I have thrown small pebbles into a very large pond, and have no way of knowing whether any pebble caused the slightest ripple. I don't need to worry about that. My responsibility was the effort"
Martha Gellhorn
Ann Clwyd, Member of Parliament, Cynon Valley

"Nothing in life is to be feared. It is only to be understood"
Marie Curie,
Ann Coffey, Member of Parliament, Stockport

"The only lost cause is the one you give up on before you start"
Vaclav Havel
Yvette Cooper, Member of Parliament, Pontefract & Castleford

"I remember as a 25 year old mother of two telling someone that I was old and didn't think much more would happen in my life. Twenty five years later to the day, I made my maiden speech in the House of Commons. There are always new beginnings"
Jean Corston, Member of Parliament, Bristol East

"Boldness be my friend! Arm me, audacity, from head to foot!"
Cymbeline, William Shakespeare
Ann Cryer, Member of Parliament, Keighley

"Keep your eyes on the prize"
American Civil Rights slogan
Roseanna Cunningham, Member of Parliament, Perth

"Unwittingly my daughters have invited me to fight a debilitating disease - discrimination.
I cannot ignore their potential nor the enormity of the task at hand but finally I shall look at them and myself and say 'I did all I could' "
Claire Curtis-Thomas, Member of Parliament, Crosby

"*Apollinaire said*   *'Come to the edge'*   *They came to the edge*
'Come to the edge'   *'We might fall'*   *He pushed them*
'It is too high'   *'Come to the edge'*   *And they flew*" Anon.

Valerie Davey, Member of Parliament, Bristol West

"How wonderful to take a break in aid of Breakthrough"
Janet Dean, Member of Parliament, Burton

"Work for a better, more just world. Accept the set-backs and celebrate each step along the way"
Julia Drown
Member of Parliament
Swindon South

" I disapprove of what you say - but I will defend to the death your right to say it!"
Voltaire

Gwyneth Dunwoody, Member of Parliament, Crewe & Nantwich

"In politics, guts is everything"
Barbara Castle
Angela Eagle, Member of Parliament, Wallasey

"Men must endure their going hence, even as their coming hither: Ripeness is all"
King Lear, William Shakespeare
Maria Eagle, Member of Parliament, Liverpool Garston

"Our future is everything
And it's just begun"
Louise Ellman, Member of Parliament, Liverpool Riverside

*"Then gently scan your brother man, Still gentler sister woman;
Tho' they may gang a kennin' wrang, To step aside is human"*
Address to the Unco' Guid, Robert Burns
Margaret Ewing, Member of Parliament, Moray

"You are your own rock,
You are your own light, fire and night,
Your beauty grows from within"
Lorna Fitzsimons, Member of Parliament, Rochdale

"Wherever there's somebody fightin' for a place to stand or decent job or helpin' hand,
Wherever somebody's strugglin' to be free, Look in their eyes Mom you'll see me"
The Ghost of Tom Joad, Bruce Springsteen
Caroline Flint, Member of Parliament, Don Valley

*"People are always blaming circumstances for what they are. I don't believe in circumstances
The people who get on in this world are the people who get up and look for the circumstances they want
and if they can't find them, they make them"*
George Bernard Shaw
Barbara Follett, Member of Parliament, Stevenage

"Infidelity does not consist in believing, or in disbelieving, it consists in professing to believe what one does not believe"
Tom Paine
Maria Fyfe, Member of Parliament, Glasgow Maryhill

"Women in public office will keep campaigning for more awareness"
Cheryl Gillan, Member of Parliament, Chesham & Amersham

"I can complain because rosebuds have thorns, or rejoice because the thornbush has a rose…it's all up to me"
Linda Gilroy, Member of Parliament, Plymouth Sutton

*"You don't have to have a big office
to have big thoughts"*
Llin Golding
Member of Parliament
Newcastle-under-Lyme

"Never think that you are any better than anyone else, or any worse.
Equality is in the mind and heart not in the wallet"
Eileen Gordon, Member of Parliament, Romford

"Good girls work hard, good girls do what they're told, good girls wait their turn.
And that's why good girls don't get ahead…but gutsy girls do"
Kate White
Teresa Gorman, Member of Parliament, Billericay

"We are all in the gutter,
but some of us are looking at the stars"
Lady Windermere's Fan
Oscar Wilde

Jane Griffiths
Member of Parliament
Reading East

*"Women debating the economy in Parliament will be listened to by women at home looking after children.
They will know it has just as much to do with them as with their husbands…Politics will be for all the people"*
The Rt Hon Harriet Harman, Member of Parliament, Camberwell & Peckham

"Challenges make you discover things about yourself that you never really knew.
They're what make the instrument stretch - what makes you go beyond the norm"
Cicely Tyson
Sylvia Heal, Member of Parliament, Halesowen & Rowley Regis

"This is the true joy in life - being used for a purpose recognised by yourself as a mighty one"
George Bernard Shaw

Patricia Hewitt, Member of Parliament, Leicester West

"Don't let power get the better of you and remember why you started out in the first place"
Margaret Hodge
Member of Parliament
Barking

"And I shall have some peace there,
For peace comes dropping slow,
Dropping from the veils of morning to where the cricket sings"
The Lake Isle of Innisfree, W B Yeats
Kate Hoey, Member of Parliament, Vauxhall

"For every Member of Parliament elected, there are many other ordinary people who, with different life chances, could serve equally well. This belief is the basis of the trust which I feel is at the heart of what being an MP is all about"

Beverley Hughes, Member of Parliament, Stretford & Urmston

"I myself have never been able to find out precisely what Feminism is; I only know that people call me a Feminist whenever I express sentiments that differentiate me from a doormat"
Rebecca West

Joan Humble, Member of Parliament, Blackpool North & Fleetwood

"Only connect"
Howards End, E.M. Forster,
Glenda Jackson, Member of Parliament, Hampstead & Highgate

53

"Where the earth beneath your feet is good and clean and sweet…"
Helen Jackson, Member of Parliament, Sheffield Hillsborough

"One clear idea is too precious a treasure to lose"
Caroline Gilman
Melanie Johnson, Member of Parliament, Welwyn Hatfield

"You can bend but never break me
'Cause it only serves to make me
More determined to achieve my final goal.

Fiona Jones, Member of Parliament, Newark

And I come back even stronger
Not a novice any longer,
'Cause you've deepened the conviction in my soul.

Oh, yes, I am wise But it's wisdom born of pain
Yes, I've paid the price But look how much I gained.
If I have to I can do anything. I am strong, I am invincible, I am woman"

I am Woman, Helen Reddy and Ray Burton

"No one can make you feel inferior without your permission"
Eleanor Roosevelt
Helen Jones, Member of Parliament, Warrington North

"Breast cancer has come out of the shadows.
When a friend of mine died from it fifteen years ago no one talked about it,
it was considered embarrassing and indelicate.
Things have changed, and I am proud to be associated with this change"
Jenny Jones, Member of Parliament, Wolverhampton South West

"… we would not have been supplied with necks if we had not been intended to stick them out occasionally"
Arthur Koestler
Lynne Jones, Member of Parliament, Birmingham Selly Oak

"Those who live for eternity are rare,
But if you care only about some transient thing
Your destiny is fearful, your house tottering !"
Osip Mandelstam

Tessa Jowell, Member of Parliament, Dulwich & West Norwood

"As women we live on in the lives of our children and the memories of our friends"
Sally Keeble, Member of Parliament, Northampton North

No coats today. Buds bulge on chestnut trees,
and on the doorstep of a big, old house
a young man plays his flute.
Ann Keen, Member of Parliament, Brentford & Isleworth

I watch the silver notes fly up
and circle in the blue sky above the traffic,
travelling where they will.

And suddenly this paving stone
mid way between my front door
and the bus stop is a starting point.

From here I can go anywhere I choose.

New Season, Wendy Cope

"With malice toward none; with charity for all; with firmness in the right, as God gives us to see the right, let us strive on to finish the work we are in"
Abraham Lincoln
Ruth Kelly, Member of Parliament, Bolton West

"I am above 80 years old; it is about time for me to be going. I have been 40 years a slave and 40 years free,
and would be here 40 years more to have equal rights for all. I suppose I am kept here because something remains for me to do;
I suppose I am yet to help to break the chain"
Sojourner Truth 19 May 1867 Speaking to the National Convention of American Equal Rights Association
Jane Kennedy, Member of Parliament, Liverpool Wavertree

"It is with the heart one sees rightly; what is essential is invisible to the eye"
Antoine de Saint Exupéry
Tess Kingham, Member of Parliament, Gloucester

"I'm sure it's more satisfying to get to the top if you start at the bottom"

Oona King
Member of Parliament
Bethnal Green & Bow

"Loveliest of trees, the cherry now
Is hung with bloom along the bough,
And stands about the woodland ride
Wearing white for Eastertide

Now, of my threescore years and ten,
Twenty will not come again,
And take from seventy springs a score,
It only leaves me fifty more,

And since to look at things in bloom,
Fifty Springs are little room,
about the woodlands I will go
To see the cherry hung with snow"

Julie Kirkbride, Member of Parliament, Bromsgrove

A Shropshire Lad, A. E. Housman

"I am a Conservative to preserve all that is good in our Constitution,
a radical to remove all that is bad. I seek to preserve property and to respect order,
and I equally decry the appeal to the passions of the many or the prejudices of the few"
Benjamin Disraeli

Eleanor Laing, Member of Parliament, Epping Forest

"Politics is not a science ... but an art"
"Politics is the art of the possible"
Bismarck
Jacqui Lait, Member of Parliament, Beckenham

"The least of things with a meaning is worth more in life than the greatest of things without it"
Carl Gustav Jung
Jackie Lawrence, Member of Parliament, Preseli Pembrokeshire

"The spiritual friendship that exists between people of integrity springs out of their common attitude to life, their shared moral outlook and the kind of activities they engage in - in other words it consists of mutual agreement in matters human and divine, combined with goodwill and practical loving concern"
Aelrich of Rievaulx

Helen Liddell, Member of Parliament, Airdrie & Shotts

"First they came for the Jews,
And I did not speak out -
Because I was not a Jew

Fiona Mactaggart, Member of Parliament, Slough

Then they came for the communists
And I did not speak out
Because I was not a communist.

Then they came for the trade unionists
And I did not speak out -
Because I was not a trade unionist.

Then they came for me -
And there was no one left
To speak out for me"

Pastor Niemöller

"You can't kill the spirit. She is like a mountain"
Alice Mahon, Member of Parliament, Halifax

"Courage is the price that life exacts for granting peace"
Amelia Earhart
Judy Mallaber, Member of Parliament, Amber Valley

"All that is necessary for evil to triumph is that good men do nothing"
Edmund Burke
Theresa May
Member of Parliament
Maidenhead

"To influence, you must love; to love, you must pray"
Communion Prayer Book, St James, Hebden Bridge
Christine McCafferty, Member of Parliament, Calder Valley

"If you really want something, work for it to happen"
Siobhain McDonagh
Member of Parliament
Mitcham & Morden

"However certain our expectation
The moment foreseen may be unexpected
When it arrives"
Murder in the Cathedral, T.S. Eliot
Anne McGuire, Member of Parliament, Stirling

"Give me the strength to serve and the grace to do so with humility"
Anne McIntosh, Member of Parliament, Vale of York

"Smile, be happy and enjoy life to the full. No-one ever choked swallowing their pride"
Shona McIsaac
Member of Parliament
Cleethorpes

"You gain strength, courage and confidence by every experience.
You must stop and look fear in the face…
You must do the things you think you cannot do"
Eleanor Roosevelt
Rosemary McKenna, Member of Parliament, Cumbernauld & Kilsyth

"Our deepest fear is not that we are inadequate. Our deepest fear is that we are powerful beyond measure. It is our light, not our darkness, that most frightens us. We ask ourselves "Who am I to be brilliant, gorgeous, talented, fabulous? Actually, who are you not to be? You are a child of God. Your playing small doesn't serve the world.

Gillian Merron, Member of Parliament, Lincoln

There is nothing enlightened about shrinking so that other people won't feel insecure around you. We were born to make manifest the glory of God that is within us. It's not just in some of us; it's in everyone. And as we let our own light shine, we unconsciously give other people permission to do the same. As we are liberated from our own fear, our presence automatically liberates others"

Nelson Mandela

"Yet still the blood is strong, the heart is Highland,
And we in dreams behold the Hebrides"
Canadian Boat Song
Ray Michie, Member of Parliament, Argyll & Bute

"As a former nurse I have decided the job as MP is very similar; long hours, plenty of ups and downs and loads of job satisfaction"
Laura Moffatt
Member of Parliament
Crawley

"Injustice anywhere is a threat to justice everywhere"
Martin Luther King
Margaret Moran, Member of Parliament, Luton South

"I want to be all that I am capable of becoming....."
Katherine Mansfield
Julie Morgan
Member of Parliament
Cardiff North

"If you are thinking ten years ahead plant a tree
If you are thinking 100 years ahead educate the people"
Kuan Tzu
Estelle Morris, Member of Parliament, Birmingham Yardley

"The problem for most women is that it is hard to be inspired when you are tired"
Kali Mountford, Member of Parliament, Colne Valley

"History despite its wrench and pain cannot be unlived.
But if faced with courage, need not be lived again"
Maya Angelou
The Rt Hon Mo Mowlam, Member of Parliament, Redcar

"Long experience has taught me that to be criticized is not always to be wrong"
Anthony Eden
Diana Organ, Member of Parliament, Forest of Dean

"I think it pisses God off if you walk by the Color Purple in a field somewhere and don't notice it"
The Color Purple, Alice Walker
"The positive things in life often pass us by"
Sandra Osborne, Member of Parliament, Ayr

"Getting used to fitting in with the background - an MP's life is a healthy challenge for a 50-year old!"
Linda Perham, Member of Parliament, Ilford North

"I think if the people of this country can be reached by the truth, their judgement will be in favour of the many, as against the privileged few"
Eleanor Roosevelt
Bridget Prentice, Member of Parliament, Lewisham East

"What do we live for, if it is not to make life less difficult for each other?"
George Eliot
Dawn Primarolo, Member of Parliament, Bristol South

"Don't care if others think you're a snook,
You can change your life with a book"
Prison Education Diaries
Joyce Quin, Member of Parliament, Gateshead East & Washington West

"This party is a moral crusade or it is nothing"
Harold Wilson
Barbara Roche,
Member of Parliament,
Hornsey & Wood Green.

"From quiet homes and first beginnings, out to the undiscovered ends
There's nothing worth the wear of winning, but laughter and the love of friends"
Dedicatory Ode, Hilaire Belloc
Marion Roe, Member of Parliament, Broxbourne

"The world would be a better place if it were governed by the women in it"
Caption mounted in pink neon lights on Dublin City Hall, as part of a student art presentation - October 1997
Joan Ruddock, Member of Parliament, Lewisham, Deptford

"May you live all the days of your life"
Jonathan Swift
Christine Russell
Member of Parliament
City of Chester

"It is a privilege to be involved with this Breakthrough project and if this book helps to prevent even one more woman suffering from Breast Cancer then it will have succeeded"
Joan Ryan, Member of Parliament, Enfield North

"Breast cancer is an individual problem, but raising awareness of it is a collective responsibility for all women"
The Rt Hon Gillian Shephard, Member of Parliament, South West Norfolk

"When I was five months pregnant my partner was diagnosed as having cancer. It made me very aware of the need to make every day count: that means something different to each of us but most definitely something to all of us"
Debra Shipley
Member of Parliament
Stourbridge

"I cannot help thinking that the amount of unfairness and poverty in the world and the absence of women in politics are connected. It isn't that women are saints but they do most of the caring for children, the sick and frail elderly. My hope is that, as women take up their place, we will create a more just order"

The Rt Hon Clare Short
Member of Parliament
Birmingham Ladywood

"Friendship with oneself is important,
because without it one cannot be
friends with anyone else in the world"
Eleanor Roosevelt

Angela Smith
Member of Parliament
Basildon

"Where there is no vision, the people perish"
Proverbs
Geraldine Smith, Member of Parliament, Morecambe & Lunesdale

"If women . . .had had their due influence from the beginning
they might have been able to prevent the existence of abuses which men socialists are now trying to get rid of"
Christabel Pankhurst
Jacqui Smith, Member of Parliament, Redditch

"I will arise and go now, for always night and day I hear lake water lapping with low sounds by the shore;
While I stand on the roadway, or on the pavements grey, I hear it in the deep heart's core"
The Lake Isle of Innisfree, W B Yeats
Helen Southworth, Member of Parliament, Warrington South

"Unless we are pro-active with more intensive screening for breast cancer
and give extra help to families genetically predisposed to suffer from this disease,
we shall all be culpable for deaths which could have been avoided"
Caroline Spelman, Member of Parliament, Meriden

"What the world needs... A little more kindness, A little less needs, A little more giving, A little less greed, A little more gladness
A little less care, A little more faith, And a little more prayer, A little more 'We,' A little less 'I'
A little more laughter, A little less sigh, A little more sunshine Brightening the view, A lot more friends Exactly like you !"
Written by a low paid, part time working woman from Northern Ireland named Maureen

Rachel Squire, Member of Parliament, Dunfermline West

"Notre vie n'a de valeur,
qu'en fonction
des efforts qu'elle nous coûte"
"The value of our lives is in the effort
that they cost"
Phyllis Starkey
Member of Parliament
Milton Keynes South West

"Do not be afraid to take a big step, you cannot cross a chasm in two small jumps"
Gisela Stuart, Member of Parliament, Birmingham Edgbaston

"You should always try to do what you want to do before you settle for anything else"
The Rt Hon Ann Taylor, Member of Parliament, Dewsbury

"When summer's end is nighing And skies at evening cloud,
I muse on change and fortunes And all the feats I vowed
When I was young and proud"
Last Poem, A.E. Housman
Dari Taylor, Member of Parliament, Stockton South

"Always tell the truth- it's easier to remember what you said. Never be afraid
to say 'I don't know' - you are never too old to learn"
Jenny Tonge, Member of Parliament, Richmond Park

*"Vision without action
is merely a dream.
Action without vision
just passes time.
Vision with action can
change the world"
The Power of Vision*
J.A. Barker
Joan Walley
Member of Parliament
Stoke-on-Trent North

"People are often concerned with age. But it doesn't matter how old or how young you are. Only whether you can do the job"
Claire Ward, Member of Parliament, Watford

*"…it is not the beginning, but the continuing of the same,
until it be thoroughly finished, which yieldeth the true glory"*
Sir Francis Drake
The Rt Hon Ann Widdecombe, Member of Parliament, Maidstone & The Weald

Betty Williams, Member of Parliament, Conwy

"I returned, and saw under the sun, that the race is not to the swift, nor the battle to the strong, neither yet bread to the wise, nor yet riches to men of understanding, nor yet favour to men of skill; but time and chance happeneth to them all"
Ecclesiastes

Ann Winterton, Member of Parliament, Congleton

"We are here to claim our right as women, not only to be free, but to fight for freedom.
That is our right as well as our duty"
Votes for Women, Dame Christabel Pankhurst

Rosie Winterton, Member of Parliament, Doncaster Central

"I grew up in a family that believed that politics is part of life and I accepted that view. When very young I looked at the world and decided it could be improved. I hated war and poverty and wanted a world in which people could develop themselves and care for each other. Most people in the street don't think an ordinary person can make a difference, but I am an ordinary person and I thimk I can. I don't think of politics as a career but as a passion"

Audrey Wise, Member of Parliament, Preston

Index of MPs

Diane Abbott MP, Hackney North & Stoke Newington, L
Irene Adams MP, Paisley North, L
Janet Anderson MP, Rossendale & Darwen, L
Hilary Armstrong MP, North West Durham, L
Candy Atherton MP, Falmouth & Camborne, L
Charlotte Atkins MP, Staffordshire Moorlands, L
Jackie Ballard MP, Taunton, LD
The Rt. Hon. Margaret Beckett MP, Derby South, L
Anne Begg MP, Aberdeen South, L
Elizabeth Blackman MP, Erewash, L
Hazel Blears MP, Salford, L
The Rt. Hon. Betty Boothroyd MP, West Bromwich West, L
The Rt. Hon. Virginia Bottomley MP, South West Surrey, C
Helen Brinton MP, Peterborough, L
Angela Browning MP, Tiverton & Honiton, C
Karen Buck MP, Regent's Park & Kensington North, L
Christine Butler MP, Castle Point, L
Anne Campbell MP, Cambridge, L
Judith Church MP, Dagenham, L
Lynda Clark, MP, Edinburgh Pentlands, L
Ann Clwyd MP, Cynon Valley, L
Ann Coffey MP, Stockport, L
Yvette Cooper MP, Pontefract & Castleford, L
Jean Corston MP, Bristol East, L
Ann Cryer MP, Keighley, L
Roseanna Cunningham MP, Perth, SNP
Claire Curtis-Thomas MP, Crosby, L
Valerie Davey MP. Bristol West, L
Janet Dean MP, Burton, L
Julia Drown MP, Swindon South, L
Gwyneth Dunwoody MP, Crewe & Nantwich, L
Angela Eagle MP, Wallasey, L
Maria Eagle MP, Liverpool Garston, L
Louise Ellman MP, Liverpool Riverside, L/C
Margaret Ewing MP, Moray, SNP
Lorna Fitzsimons MP, Rochdale, L
Caroline Flint MP, Don Valley, L
Barbara Follett MP, Stevenage, L
Maria Fyfe MP, Glasgow Maryhill, L
Cheryl Gillan MP, Chesham & Amersham, C
Linda Gilroy MP, Plymouth Sutton, L/C

Llin Golding MP, Newcastle-under-Lyme, L
Eileen Gordon MP, Romford, L
Teresa Gorman MP, Billericay, C
Jane Griffiths MP, Reading East, L
The Rt. Hon. Harriet Harman MP, Camberwell & Peckham, L
Sylvia Heal MP, Halesowen & Rowley Regis, L
Patricia Hewitt MP, Leicester West, L
Margaret Hodge MP, Barking, L
Kate Hoey MP, Vauxhall, L
Beverley Hughes MP, Stretford & Urmston, L
Joan Humble MP, Blackpool North & Fleetwood, L
Glenda Jackson MP, Hampstead & Highgate, L
Helen Jackson MP, Sheffield Hillsborough, L
Melanie Johnson MP, Welwyn Hatfield, L
Fiona Jones MP, Newark, L
Helen Jones MP, Warrington North, L
Jenny Jones MP, Wolverhampton South-West , L
Lynne Jones MP, Birmingham Selly Oak, L
Tessa Jowell MP, Dulwich & West Norwich, L
Sally Keeble MP, Northampton North, L
Ann Keen MP, Brentford & Isleworth, L
Ruth Kelly MP, Bolton West, L
Jane Kennedy MP, Liverpool Wavertree, L
Tess Kingham MP, Gloucester, L
Oona King MP, Bethnal Green & Bow, L
Julie Kirkbride MP, Bromsgrove, C
Eleanor Laing MP, Epping Forrest, C
Jacqui Lait MP, Beckenham, C
Jackie Lawrence MP, Preseli Pembrokshire, L
Helen Liddell MP, Airdrie & Shotts, L
Fiona Mactaggart MP, Slough, L
Alice Mahon MP, Halifax, L
Judy Mallaber MP, Amber Valley, L
Theresa May MP, Maidenhead, C
Christine McCafferty MP, Calder Valley, L
Siobhain McDonagh MP, Mitcham & Morden, L
Anne McGuire MP, Stirling, L
Anne McIntosh MP, Vale of York, L
Shona McIsaac MP, Cleethorpes, L
Rosemary McKenna MP, Cumbernauld & Kilsyth, L
Gillian Merron MP, Lincoln, L

Ray Michie MP, Argyll & Bute, LD
Laura Moffatt MP, Crawley, L
Margaret Moran MP, Luton South, L
Julie Morgan MP, Cardiff North, L
Estelle Morris MP, Birmingham Yardley, L
Kali Mountford MP, Colne Valley, L
The Rt. Hon. Marjorie Mowlam MP, Redcar, L
Diana Organ MP, Forest of Dean, L
Sandra Osborne MP, Ayr, L
Linda Perham MP, Ilford North, L
Bridget Prentice MP, Lewisham East, L
Dawn Primarolo MP, Bristol South, L
Joyce Quin MP, Gateshead East & Washington West, L
Barbara Roche MP, Hornsey & Wood Green, L
Marion Roe MP, Broxbourne, C
Joan Ruddock MP, Lewisham, Deptford, L
Christine Russell MP, City of Chester, L
Joan Ryan MP, Enfield North, L
The Rt. Hon. Gillian Shephard MP, Norfolk South West, C
Debra Shipley MP, Stourbridge, L
The Rt. Hon. Clare Short MP, Birmingham Ladywood, L
Angela Smith MP, Basildon, L/C
Geraldine Smith MP, Morecambe & Lunesdale, L
Jacqui Smith MP, Redditch, L
Helen Southworth MP, Warrington South, L
Caroline Spelman MP, Meriden, C
Rachel Squire MP, Dunfermline West, L
Phyllis Starkey MP, Milton Keynes South West, L
Gisela Stuart MP, Birmingham Edgbaston, L
The Rt. Hon. Ann Taylor MP, Dewsbury, L
Dari Taylor MP, Stockton South, L
Jenny Tonge MP, Richmond Park, LD
Joan Walley MP, Stoke-on-Trent North, L
Claire Ward MP, Watford, L
The Rt. Hon. Ann Widdecombe MP, Maidstone & The Weald, C
Betty Williams MP, Conwy, L
Ann Winterton MP, Congleton, C
Rosie Winterton MP, Doncaster Central, L
Audrey Wise MP, Preston, L

Dianne Abbott was unable to take part in this publication

C Conservative   L Labour   L/C Labour/Co-op   LD Liberal Democrat   SNP Scottish National Party